William Fiddian Moulton

The Bible as Literature

William Fiddian Moulton

The Bible as Literature

ISBN/EAN: 9783337171919

Printed in Europe, USA, Canada, Australia, Japan

Cover: Foto ©Lupo / pixelio.de

More available books at **www.hansebooks.com**

No. 1   Fifteen Cents

New Education
In the Church Series

—

The Bible
as Literature

—

W. Fiddian Moulton, M.A.

St. John's College, Cambridge

—

1895
MEADVILLE PENNA:
FLOOD & VINCENT
The Chautauqua=Century Press

The

Bible as Literature

BY

W. FIDDIAN MOULTON, M.A.

St. John's College, Cambridge

MEADVILLE, PENNA:
FLOOD AND VINCENT
The Chautauqua-Century Press
1895

The Chautauqua-Century Press, Meadville, Pa., U. S. A.
Electrotyped, Printed, and Bound by Flood & Vincent.

PREFACE.

By Professor R. G. Moulton, of the University of Chicago.

I HAVE been requested to say a few words as preface to this little book, written by my nephew, on the Bible as literature. The title is a wide one : but I think the writer is well advised in confining himself to the side of literary treatment most urgently required in the case of sacred literature, and explaining, with as much clearness as the brief limits permit, the chief forms of literature contained in the Bible and Apocrypha.

The question is often asked, What is exactly meant by the term "literary study" in application to Scripture ? There can be no better way of answering this question than to take a specific portion of the Bible, and illustrate the literary treatment in comparison with other and familiar modes of study.

Let the reader refresh his memory by reading the twenty-fourth psalm. He will feel no difficulty in understanding how this portion of Scripture would be handled by the religious or theological student. The psalm would be read through as a devotional exercise, perhaps with responsive reading. Again, the early verses would make a text for a sermon on purity as a condition for worship ; the later verses might be applied to the celebration of an article of the creed—the Ascent of Christ into Heaven.

Another treatment of the psalm would be the historic analysis, now usually associated with the "higher criticism." A critic of this order would, in the case of the twenty-fourth psalm, be especially struck with the break in the poem at the end of the sixth verse, by which the two halves of the psalm seem totally dissimilar in matter and style. With his special bias to find the solution of all difficulties in historic considerations, the "higher critic" would lay down that we have here, not one psalm, but two : the later verses having the dramatic form that suggests poetry of an early age, the first six verses exhibiting the reflective style of later literature ; while the combination of the two in one must be the mistake of some transcriber or editor.

The purely literary student would have a

purpose different from either of the two described so far. He would approach the psalm with the inquiry, Where are we to place this in a classification of literary forms? Is it epic, lyric, dramatic, or what? A little study would lead him to classify both portions of the psalm with "Occasional Odes," or better, as "Anthems." Having got so far, he would naturally ask whether the difference between the two anthems might not be explained by their connection with varying portions of some ceremonial occasion. This occasion is easily found in the Inauguration of Jerusalem by David, when the ark was escorted in solemn procession from its resting place in the hill country to the newly captured fortress (2 *Samuel* vi.). The first six verses make an anthem to be sung as the procession halts at the foot of the hill on which the city stands ; hence the relevancy of its inquiry, "Who shall *ascend* into the hill of the LORD?" The latter part of the psalm is the crowning anthem of the ceremony, performed in front of the ancient gates of the fortress. Hence its military and dramatic form : a summons of the city to receive its King, answered by a challenge of the warders from within.

Army—Lift up your heads, O ye gates,   .   .   .
      That the King of Glory may come in.
Warders—Who is the King of Glory?

Thus the two anthems that make up the psalm fit into the two parts of the day's ceremonial, as a key fits into the wards of a lock.

Why is it that this "literary study of the Bible" is only just now coming to be a prominent topic of discussion? The answer is simple. The literary character of Holy Scripture has always been familiar to those who read in the Hebrew and Greek, but the English reader was excluded from it until the publication of the Revised Version. The Authorized Version is full of beauty, but its beauties are all of single verses. Its translators thought of little beyond giving readers stores of "good words"; its unintelligent division into chapters and verses makes a monotony of form under which all literary structure—of songs, sonnets, dramatic dialogue, essay, discourse—lies buried; when the reader of this translation desires to understand the connectedness of thought, he must go to the original languages to find out what his English version means. Accordingly, to the great majority of readers, the

Bible is no more than isolated verses, isolated texts : as if the Bible were a divine scrapbook. The Revised Version makes it possible for a mere English reader to go through the book of *Job*, and by himself follow all of its drift and turns of argument ; in the historical books the Revised Version makes clear to his eye when Moses or Balaam breaks out into poetry ; even in *Solomon's Song* he can see that he is reading poetic dialogue. Whether it is wholesome even in religious study to rest upon texts apart from context is a serious question. But it is a certainty that the reader who desires to appreciate the literary beauty of the Bible must do his reading in the Revised Version.

R. G. MOULTON.

INTRODUCTION.

FOR this brief account of the literary aspect of the Bible no better motto, perhaps, can be selected than Lord Macaulay's celebrated saying that the Bible is a "well of English, pure and undefiled"; for in these words lies the recognition, by one who was himself one of the very greatest masters of the English tongue, that the Bible has a literary as well as a religious *raison d'être*. And this may well be the case without impairing in the slightest degree its supreme position as the keystone of the Christian religion. Not once, nor twice, but times without number have men come to this well to draw, and have found one sitting there who has spoken to them, as man never spake, concerning God, and life, and duty; and they, who came only to drink of this well of English undefiled, have gone away with their thirst quenched with the Water of Life. There is involved, therefore, no conflict between the literary and the spiritual study of the Bible : for all genuine study, from either standpoint, must result in in-

creased appreciation of its spiritual value;
and the same method of study which is essential for a true appreciation of its literary
beauty—namely, consecutive and compre-
hensive study, as opposed to concentration
upon isolated texts—is equally essential for
the full understanding of its spiritual teaching. When this is adopted, the Bible will be
realized to be at the same time a storehouse
of religious instruction and a library of literary masterpieces. In it there are contained
specimens of all the fundamental types of
literature which we are accustomed to recog-
nize to-day, and moreover the types are to
be found in their highest expression. This
will become more clear if I sum up concisely
the subject matter of the Bible, and then pro-
ceed to show how all the various literary types
within its limits serve to illustrate and enforce its central facts.

The Bible is the record of the dealings of
God with one small section of the human
race, which He had selected as the medium
for His revelation of Himself to the race.
This purpose necessarily involves the record-
ing of yet more primitive times before the
differentiation of this family had taken place;
but the whole record is shaped with this

end in view, and whatever is said concerning other races is only introduced in so
far as it bears upon the fortunes of the
chosen people. The development of that
people is traced through the successive
stages of patriarchal, theocratic, and mon-
archic government; until after a long and
checkered period of probation they reach
the point at which the time is ripe for the
final consummation of the revelation up to
which everything has tended in the long and
varied past, and with that revelation, in the
person of the Messiah and in the teaching of
his immediate followers, the Bible closes.

Such is, in very brief terms, the central
historical framework upon which the sacred
writings hang, and which in their turn they
elucidate and verify; to use another figure of
speech, if the above historical record of the
Bible be the stem of the tree, then the rest of
the Scriptures are the branches and the
leaves, in vital connection with the stem, and
contributing beauty and completeness to its
growth. Take, for instance, the book of
Genesis, where there are eleven chapters of
chronicle, containing just two or three epi-
sodes told in detail, followed by thirty-nine
chapters dealing with patriarchal authority

and customs, and dealing with them, not in
the matter-of-fact style of a chronicler, but
after the manner of a poet who would fain
impress his message upon the imagination.
From the standpoint of pure history this
would show grievous want of proportion :
the historical requirements for these patriarchal pictures would be little more than
half a dozen chapters; why fill thirty-nine?
Because the grafting of this epic element
on to the chronicle is invaluable for the purpose of forcing home the lesson which lies
beneath the whole of the Bible record, and
which the bare record would fail to drive
home.

Again, what bare chronicle, what elaborate history even—told from outside—could
give the insight into the inner relations
between God and His people that is afforded
by the lyrics of the book of *Psalms*, or the
oratory of the book of *Deuteronomy?* Each
one of these literary forms is particularly
adapted for the purpose to which it is put ;
and, whether by image or song, episode or
oration, the main purpose of the book is
ever being carried out, of revealing the will
of God to man. The five main literary
types may be differentiated as History,

Lyrics, Philosophy, Prophecy, and Parable; but it will easily be seen that the types are apt to approach each other very closely at times, and that a work may well manifest some of the characteristics of two types. The book of *Job*, for instance, affords examples of most of the types, while the *Song of Solomon* does not fall easily within any of the classes. Nevertheless, for general purposes this classification will serve very well.

The Bible as Literature.

CHAPTER I.

HISTORY.

THE historical matter in the Bible is both great in quantity and various in kind. There is, firstly, the historical frame-work referred to above, which Historical framework. runs through the whole volume and must be distinguished from the epic incidents. The book of *Genesis* opens with the barest chronicle of the beginnings of the world and some few epic* incidents merged in it, such as the Fall, the death of Abel, the Flood, and the building of the Tower of Babel. With the entrance of Abraham (chapter xii.) the whole character of the narrative changes: cycles of Epic incidents. stories, centering in Abraham, Isaac, Jacob, and Joseph, take the place of the chronicle, and from this point onward the epic element is predominant. A few

---

* The word "epic" must not be confused with "fiction": it merely implies that the events are told in a manner that appeals to imagination and sympathy, and not, like history, merely to the sense of record.

instances will suffice to make this plain. Between verses 6 and 7 of *Exodus* i., a period elapses sufficient to permit of the Hebrew tribe reaching the proportions of a menacing foe, and yet there is no chronicle extant of the period. Likewise the bulk of the judgeship of Samuel is pressed into three verses (1 *Sam.* vii. 15–17), and the long reigns of Jeroboam II. and Uzziah have each to be content with seven verses (2 *Kings* xiv. 23–29; xv. 1–7). In face of this it can scarcely be maintained that the historical books of the Bible are more than an historical framework with epic incidents merged in them. Of the vividness of many of these epic incidents it is hard to speak too strongly; and the effect is heightened when, as in the story of Balaam, prose gives place to verse at each successive climax.

The third element of the historical literature of the Bible is what may be styled either ecclesiastical or constitutional history. Not that the terms are ordinarily interchangeable, but the peculiar character of the Hebrew state renders them so. Israel had no law save its Mosaic code, no constitution save that of its church, and hence its ecclesiastical

Ecclesiastical or constitutional history.

history is constitutional, and its constitutional ecclesiastical. To this class belong a considerable portion of *Exodus* and *Numbers* and practically all of *Leviticus*, which deal with the minute regulations laid down for the performance of duties towards man and towards God. The books of *Chronicles*, if not so completely ecclesiastical in their subject matter, are thoroughly so in their treatment ; and in like manner the books of *Ezra* and *Nehemiah* deal with the history of the church as restored after the Exile. The Gospels may, in a sense, be placed in this class also, for they are historical, but at the same time they are prophetic, because embodying, in the highest degree, the divine message which constitutes the essence of prophecy.

CHAPTER II.

IN DEALING with the lyric literature of the Bible we are immediately faced by the difficulty which arises from the different criteria for verse in Hebrew and in English. We are accustomed to associate distinct and more or less regular meter with verse, and in ordinary parlance we make no distinction between poetry and verse. Now, for the appreciation of the literary forms of the Bible both these preconceived ideas must be abandoned. To take the smaller question first, poetry is not dependent for its existence upon meter or rhythm or any characteristic of external form, but signifies primarily a creation, as distinguished from mere discussion of what already exists. Thus poetry may be pure fiction or it may be based upon a foundation of fact, worked upon by the imagination; but in either case it is differentiated by its spirit and not by its form. The distinction between Hebrew verse and English verse is more essential for our purpose, as we shall look in vain in the Bible for verse after the English pattern, since Hebrew verse is distinguished from prose not by syllabic meter but by structural parallelism.

> Thy word is a lamp unto my feet,
> And light unto my path.

This often has the effect of much weakening the distinction between prose and verse, in that parallelism is a recognized feature in the rhetorical prose of all languages, and the study of the particular passage as a whole must be depended upon for making clear whether it is to be regarded as prose or verse.

The lyrics of the Bible fall under six main heads, the *Song of Solomon* forming a seventh and standing by itself.

First may be considered the elegies: though here as elsewhere care must be taken not to associate with the idea the Elegies. same strictness which we associate with elegiacs in Latin. The Hebrew elegy, at first a dirge or lament, ultimately loses this exclusive character and comes to be the expression of powerful emotion of any kind. Of elegies in the stricter sense the most notable examples are the lamentations of Jeremiah, David's lament over Saul (2 *Sam.* i.) and Psalm cxxxvii.

Hymns of worship are, of course, largely represented in the Bible, and present considerable variety both in form and matter. They may be classified under the heads of general thanksgiving, specific thanksgiving, and private meditations. The third class is naturally the least elaborate in form; or, to speak more accurately, the form has an elaborateness of its own, acrostics—*e. g.*, Psalm cxix.—taking the place of the antiphonal singing which was so prominent a feature of Jewish worship from the days of Moses and Miriam, Deborah and Barak, onwards. Of perfectly general thanksgivings the final section of the book of *Psalms* (cxlv.–cl.) may serve as a typical example ; to which may be added the twin psalms, so to speak, both singing of ever-watchful providence in the sphere of human life (ciii.) and external nature (civ.). The Songs of Ascents (cxx.–cxxxiv.) must be classed among the specific thanksgivings, as having reference to pilgrimages or other specific occasions, although there is no trace of agreement among scholars as to the precise signification of the title. Psalm cxviii. evi-

Hymns of worship.

dently has reference to some special visit to the temple, and seems to take the form of dialogue, as the subjoined arrangement will suggest.

PSALM CXVIII.

The Worshipper and His Escort approach the Temple.

Tutti.	O give thanks unto the Lord ; for he is good : For his mercy endureth forever.
Worshipper.	Let Israel now say—
Escort.	That his mercy endureth forever.
Worshipper.	Let the house of Aaron now say—
Escort.	That his mercy endureth forever.
Worshipper.	Let them now that fear the Lord say—
Escort.	That his mercy endureth forever.
Worshipper.	Out of my distress I called upon the Lord : The Lord answered me, and set me in a large place. The Lord is on my side, I will not fear : What can man do unto me? The Lord is on my side with them that help me : Therefore shall I see my desire upon them that hate me.
Escort.	It is better to trust in the Lord Than to put confidence in man ;

It is better to trust in the Lord
Than to put confidence in princes.

Worshipper.   All nations compassed me about:
Escort.   In the name of the Lord I will cut
them off!
Worshipper.   They compassed me about;
Yea, they compassed me about:
Escort.   In the name of the Lord I will cut
them off!
Worshipper.   They compassed me about like bees;
They are quenched as the fire of
thorns:
Escort.   In the name of the Lord I will cut
them off!

Worshipper.   Thou didst thrust sore at me that I
might fall:
But the Lord helped me.
The Lord is my strength and song;
And he is become my salvation.
The voice of rejoicing and salvation
is in the tents of the righteous:
The right hand of the Lord doeth
valiantly.
Escort.   The right hand of the Lord is exalted:
The right hand of the Lord doeth
valiantly.
Worshipper.   I shall not die, but live,
And declare the works of the Lord.
The Lord hath chastened me sore:
But he hath not given me over unto
death.
Open to me the gates of righteous-
ness:

> I will enter into them,
> I will give thanks unto the Lord.

The Temple Gates open and disclose a Chorus of
Priests.

Priests. This is the Gate of the Lord :
The righteous shall enter into it.

Worshipper. I will give thanks unto thee, for thou
hast answered me,
And art become my salvation.
The stone which the builders re-
jected
Is become the head of the corner.

Escort. This is the Lord's doing ;
It is marvelous in our eyes.
This is the day which the Lord hath
made ;
We will rejoice and be glad in it.
Save now, we beseech thee, O Lord :
O Lord, we beseech thee, send now
prosperity.

The Worshipper enters the Temple : the Escort pre-
pare to retire.

Priests (to the Worshipper).

Blessed be he that entereth in the
name of the Lord !

(to the Escort retiring).

We have blessed you out of the
house of the Lord !

Priests. The Lord is God, and he hath given
us light :
Bind the sacrifice with cords, even
unto the horns of the altar.

Worshipper. Thou art my God, and I will give
    thanks unto thee :
    Thou art my God, I will exalt thee.

Tutti. O give thanks unto the Lord ; for
    he is good :
    For his mercy endureth forever.

One more example must be quoted because
of its perfect rhythmic structure, and that
is Psalm cvii., the Song of the Redeemed.
The psalm has an invocation (verses 1-3),
an epilogue (verses 33-42), and four sections, each closing with the refrain, "Oh,
that men would praise the Lord for his
goodness and for his wonderful works to the
children of men," a further commentary being added in each case to suit the experience
which has just been described. But on closer
examination it will be seen that the four
sections, verses 4-9, 10-16, 17-22, 23-32,
do not simply answer each other after the
manner of strophe and anti-strophe, for the
first and fourth go together and the second
and third. In other words, the thought-
rhythm of the sections—as is the case in
the meter of Tennyson's *In Memoriam*—is
a b b a, not *a b a b*. The first and fourth
tell of misfortune and restoration, the second
and third of rebellion, discipline, and resto-

ration when the discipline has done its work.

The various odes* upon special occasions which are found in the Bible do not differ perhaps essentially from the hymns of worship noticed above, except that they are not composed primarily from the standpoint of worship. To take a modern parallel : the opening stanzas of *In Memoriam* are often included in hymn·books of the present day, and very appropriately, too; but this is not, of course, a hymn in the same sense as those among which it is found, being, rather, a special ode. Of these Biblical odes those that naturally occur first to the mind are the various Songs of Deliverance, such as the Song of Deborah (*Judges* v.), the Song of Moses and Miriam (*Exodus* xv.), David's Song of Thanksgiving (2 *Sam.* xxii. ; *Psalm* xviii.), and Psalms xlvi. and xlviii., both ot which may very possibly have reference to the destruction of the host of Sennacherib. Other odes may be associated with specific ceremonies; for example, there is much to suggest that Psalms xxiv., xxx., lxviii., and cxxxii. all formed part of the actual—or a

Odes upon special occasions.

---

* The " ode " is not a definite term; but is used for song in its highest form.

commemorative—ceremonial of bringing the ark to Jerusalem. As occasional odes of a private, not national, character may be mentioned the Song of Hannah (1 *Sam.* ii.), the Song of Habakkuk (*Hab.* iii.), and the Songs of Mary, Zacharias, and Simeon (*Luke* i. and ii.).

Of drama, in the strict sense of the word, there is none in the Bible, but there are numerous lyrics which are essentially dramatic in character, in that they represent changes of situation, which, however, are not related from without in the form of a narrative, but unfold themselves. This will be illustrated by an analysis of Psalm cxxxix. In the opening verses the psalmist is oppressed with the sense of the omniscience and omnipresence of God; he would fain escape, but he knows not whither to go for he finds God everywhere. And as the natural world is laid bare to the eye of God, so is man's inner nature, not one single element coming into existence without His knowledge, nor continuing to exist without His watchful care. This "obverse side of omniscience," so to speak, creates a revulsion of feeling, so strong that the psalmist, instead of regarding God as a

Dramatic lyrics.

rigid taskmaster, proclaims himself His ally,
and the psalm, which opened with half-petu-
lant, "Lord, thou hast searched me," ends
with an eager, " Search me, O God."

Under the title "Historical Odes" are included those lyrics—*e. g.*, Psalms lxxviii., cv.,
and cvi. and *Deuteronomy* xxxii.
—which give, as it were, a bird's-
eye view of the national history,
<small>Historical odes.</small>
and constitute an appeal to the nation to re-
view the past in the interest of the present
and the future. This poetic presentation of
history naturally allows of great latitude in
the matter of detail. Psalms cv. and cvi.
present an intelligible sequence of events to the
end of the wanderings, or perhaps to the cap-
tivity, and Psalm lxxviii. does the same, bringing the history down to the days of David.
In Psalm lxxviii. the history is presented in a
rhythmic succession of manifestations of human frailty followed by divine interposition. In
Deuteronomy xxxii., on the other hand, the
knowledge of the historical facts is assumed,
and the ode is a philosophical reflection upon
them. To this a fine parallel is to be seen in
Mr. Matthew Arnold's *Obermann Once
More*.

Separate from the above must be considered

odes like *Genesis* xxvii. 27-29, 39-40, *Deuter-*
onomy xxxiii., and the prophecies
Prophetic   of Balaam in *Numbers* xxii.–xxiv.
odes.
They partake somewhat of the
nature of oracular responses, with the neces-
sary difference which must arise from the cir-
cumstances of their origin. They are often
riddles, but the element of obscurity and
ambiguity is incidental rather than essential;
and the blessing of Moses and the orations
of Balaam do not confine themselves to the
foretelling of the future, but also give counsel
for the present.

Of the *Song of Solomon* it is extremely
difficult to speak with any confidence, either
as to its meaning or its literary
The *Song of*   form. It has a large lyric element,
Solomon.
and it presents the main characteristic of dramatic poetry, namely, story un-
folded in dialogue and action; and yet it is
neither an ode nor a drama of the ordinary
kind. There is not any opportunity here of
discussing the structure of the book in detail,
and no more can be said than that the
theory which presents fewest difficulties is
that which regards it as a series of pictures,
or idyls, all having their center in the wooing
of a certain Shulammite; but whether she is

wooed by a humble lover, who has King Solomon for his rival, or by King Solomon, under the disguise of a humble lover, cannot be argued here.*

* For this and for so many other knotty points in connection with this subject, reference should be made to Dr. R. G. Moulton's forthcoming *Literary Study of the Bible* (D. C. Heath & Co., Boston).

CHAPTER III.

PHILOSOPHY.

ALTHOUGH this branch of Bible literature has perfectly distinct characteristics of its own, it is far from easy to find at all a satisfactory name for it. By "philosophy" is generally denoted the sum total of the laws which govern mental, moral, and physical existence, those laws being first arrived at by observation and then reduced to system, the term "science" being more commonly, though not exclusively, used when dealing with the phenomena of physical existence. What biology is to physical life the wisdom literature of the Bible is to moral life; it states and systematizes the dictates of morality. It differs from prophecy in not pretending to the solemnity of a divine message, but only embodying the reflections of the wise.

The germ from which the whole of this species of literature is developed
The proverb. is the proverb, or wise saying. Its form is usually that of a couplet, the

second section of which reaffirms the first,
either directly or by contrast, e. g.:

a. The liberal soul shall be made fat,
And he that watereth shall be watered also him-
self. (Prov. xi. 25.)
b. He that is surety for a stranger shall smart for it,
But he that hateth suretiship is sure.
(Prov. xi. 15.)

It is worthy of note that the vast majority
of the Biblical proverbs are in the form of a
couplet, as above, whereas in English the
tendency is just the other way. This must
be put down to that Hebrew predilection for
parallelism which has been referred to already. Sometimes the couplet takes the
form of a simile, thus presenting two or
more sets of ideas instead of only one, e. g.:

As snow in summer and as rain in harvest,
So honour is not seemly for a fool.
(Prov. xxvi. i.)

Between the simple proverb-couplet and
the essay must be noticed the proverb-cluster
and the expanded proverb. Both Proverb-
differ from the simple proverb in cluster and
expanded
their tendency towards system- proverb.
atized thought. In the proberb-cluster
(unlike the essay) it is always possible
to conceive of a portion of the matter

being removed without a gap being necessarily discernible in the general sense
of the passage. An example may be seen
in *Proverbs* xxvi. 3-12, a cluster of sayings
on Fools. Expanded proverbs of a very
rhythmic type are to be found among the
words of Agur (*Prov.* xxx.). And if "three"
be read for "them" in xxx. 7—as is required not only by the parallelism with the
other clusters but also by the fact of three
things, not two, being specified—the balance
is most perfect :

> Two things have I asked of thee :
> Deny me not three before I die :
> Remove far from me vanity and lies :
>> Give me neither poverty nor riches :
>>> Feed me with the food that is needful for me,
>>> Lest I be full and deny thee, and say, Who is
>>> the Lord ?
>> Or lest I be poor and steal,
> And use profanely the name of my God.

The species of wisdom literature which has
been styled "essay" must be compared, not
with the highly elaborated essays of Lord
Macaulay, but rather with the dissertations
which form the chapters of Thomas à Kempis's
De Imitatione Christi, or with the essays of
Francis Bacon, concerning which the author
says : "They of all my other workes, have

beene most currant : For that, as it seemes, they come home, to Men's Busi- nesse and Bosomes." The Biblical essay differs from the proverb-cluster in the strong organic union which characterizes the former, every clause contributing its own essential portion to the argument. As an example take *St. James* ii. 1-13: On Respect of Persons.

But this section of Biblical literature is peculiarly incapable of being studied apart from actual examples; and as the examples are naturally too long for quotation, the various books in which the "wisdom" of the Bible is embodied must receive some individual attention.* Unlike the other literary types the "wisdom" of the Bible is almost exclusively contained in a few books instead of being distributed among many, those books being *Proverbs, Ecclesiastes,* the *Epistle of St. James,* and apocryphal books of *Ecclesiasticus* and *Wisdom.*

Each of these books has its own characteristics. In the book of *Proverbs* the maxims are, as the title suggests, mostly in the simple form,

---

* Macmillan & Co. announce a series of books of wisdom (*Proverbs, Ecclesiasticus, Ecclesiastes,* with *Wisdom of Solomon* and *Job*) : each of the four published in a separate volume, edited in modern literary form by Professor R. G. Moulton.

even proverb-clusters being few in number ; indeed, the only passages showing any considerable degree of elaboration are the dramatic monologues in which wisdom personified makes her appeal to the sons of men (i. 20–33 ; viii. 4–36).

Ecclesiasticus resembles *Proverbs* in that the maxims contained in them both are those which bear upon the ordinary, practical matters of daily life. But in the apocryphal book essays and proverb-clusters to a great extent supplant the simple proverb; and it moreover presents a new element in the oration upon the works of the Lord (xlii. 15–xliii.), and the well-known Panegyric upon Famous Men, from Enoch to Simon, son of Onias (xliv.–l. 24). *Ecclesiastes* opens up a new phase of "wisdom," for throughout it attempts to arrive at what is scarcely hinted at in the above-mentioned works—a philosophy of life as a whole ; and the single maxims and the essays alike are only introduced as contributions towards the formation of that philosophy.

The book of *Wisdom* shares with *Ecclesiastes* the characteristic of being an effort towards a philosophy of life as a whole; though the standpoint is different, and the maxims find expression in sustained discourses instead of a series of sorrowful or indignant outbursts. But with chapter x. comes a very marked change, and for the remainder of the book wisdom personified, very much in our sense of Providence, is pictured as watching over the successive stages of the history of the chosen people, the narrative repeatedly going off into digressions, one of which—the discourse on the folly of idolatry (chapter xiii.–xv.)—is particularly full of literary beauty. The wonderful imaginative power of this book will best be realized by comparisons of its treatment of topics with the treatment of the same topics in other writings. Take, for example, the favorite Jewish problem of the righteous in adversity as dealt with in Psalm lxxiii., and then turn to *Wisdom* v. where the inmost hearts of the arrogant are unveiled. A similar comparison may with advantage be instituted between the story of the plague of darkness as given in *Exodus* x. 21–23 and in *Wisdom* xvii.

CHAPTER IV.

PROPHECY.

IT MAY be conceded at once that the prophetic literature of the Bible belongs to a type which has no direct analogy in modern literature, and which is differentiated by its matter—and by only one characteristic of that—and not by its form. The great essential feature which marks off Biblical prophecy from all other writings is that it is the direct embodiment of the divine message, spoken "in divers portions and in divers manners through the prophets." That the possible varieties of literary form in this branch are few will easily be realized, but the body of prophetic writings is second to none in importance and in force.

At the very outset prophecy falls into two main sections, following the two distinct meanings of the Greek word from which it is derived. The Greek conception of a prophet was of a man who interpreted the will of the gods to

Two phases of prophecy.

men; and, as the message so often told concerning the future, the modern meaning of the
word crept in beside the original, but the
essence of the prophet's function was "forth-
telling," rather than "foretelling." The
Elizabethan use of "prophesying," as syn-
onymous with "preaching," reflects the
same ambiguity. Thus Biblical prophecy
falls under the two heads of preaching and
prediction, the two being at times so close
as to be incapable of separation, though at
others they are perfectly distinct. The
preaching of righteousness, which
was always so important an element The prophet
in the prophet's mission, finds its as preacher.
prototype in the magnificent orations of
Moses as given in *Deuteronomy* (i. 6 to
iv. 40; v. 1. to xi. 32; xxviii; xxix. 2 to
xxxi. 8.); but the same class of inspired
rhetoric is to be found in all the books associated with the names of the prophets. But
prophetic utterances are very far from being
all cast alike in this simple mould. Some take
the form of dialogues, others are contained
in dreams, visions, or parables—these last are
so characteristic a mode of expressing thought
in Hebrew literature as to call for separate treatment. Others, as the message of

Joel, call into requisition several literary forms, the better to enforce the word of the Lord. The prophecy of Joel opens with a dramatic lyric depicting the desolation of the land and the impending doom. A trumpet-blast announces that the day of the Lord has come, and His vengeance is working through the agency of the nations, when, by a sudden transition (ii. 12), an opportunity for repentance is held forth: "Who knoweth whether he will not turn and repent, and leave a blessing behind him." The opportunity is seized, a solemn assembly is convened, and amid national humiliation the Lord is besought to have mercy upon His people. Then follows the restoration of the nation to favor, with assurances of renewed worldly prosperity. But the restoration is not to stop at the point of giving back what had been lost: Israel is told again of a lofty spiritual mission lying before it, and again the "day of the Lord" is spoken of, no longer, however, as a terror to Israel, but as the season when it shall reap the harvest of the gentiles. Such a production as the message of *Joel* is far too irregular and abrupt in its transitions to admit of its being classified under any of the recognized literary forms ; it bears the same relation to them as Liszt's rhapsodies do to Beethoven's sonatas. The book of *Joel* partakes essentially of the two characteristics of prophecy: the prophet has his message for the present, and it does its work; but he has The prophet as foreteller. also his message concerning the future, both of Israel and of the other nations of the earth. A great proportion of this section of prophetic literature is occupied with messages of judgment against the various nations which had oppressed Israel, but Israel itself does not all escape without its own portion of denunciation. It must also be remembered that the books of the prophets contain a large element of history, introduced mainly for the purpose of making logically intelligible the messages which are sent.

CHAPTER V.

PARABLE.

ONE of the most noticeable of the general characteristics of Hebrew literature is the predilection manifested for imparting and receiving instruction by picture, image, and parable; and the amount and variety of literature of this class is so great as to justify its being treated by itself, although there must of necessity be some overlapping between this and the other classes that have been noticed. That this wealth of image-literature is due to a permanent mental characteristic is not only shown by its profusion, but also by its appearing when, most of all, direct speech was to be expected. To quote two well-known examples : when Nathan is sent to reprove David for his sin he comes with a parable upon his lips; and when Ahijah is sent to acquaint Jeroboam of the dignity in store for him he delivers his message in an acted parable, tearing his new cloak into twelve pieces and giving Jeroboam ten of them.

This class of literature falls naturally into three classes: the parable, the prophetic vision, and the book of *Job*. About the ordinary parable little *Parable.* need be said, for the teaching of Jesus has made it one of the most familiar of all literary forms. It is a mistake, however, to regard the parable as at all an exclusively New Testament method of instruction. The parable of the trees (*Judges*, ix.), of the ewe-lamb (2 *Samuel*, xii.), of the vineyard (*Isaiah*, v.), may be cited as examples of Old Testament parables.

Far more complicated is the literature which falls under the head of prophetic visions. A moment's thought will bring to mind instances of Prophetic visions. prophetic messages given, not in the form of direct address, but in dreams and visions of the night, all taking parabolic shape. It was by such parabolic vision that Peter was prepared for the great lesson he had to learn concerning the gentiles (*Acts* x. 9–16), and it was by the interpretation of such visions that both Joseph and Daniel rose to positions of influence in their respective courts. Slightly different from these visions and yet belonging to the same class is what may be styled "emblem prophecy," the teaching of a lesson not by an imaginary picture but by reference to a visible object serving as text. Under the Old Testament dispensation the ceremonial of the scapegoat was a living parable, which will serve as an example of this medium for prophetic instruction ; other examples are to be found in the girdle (*Jer.* xiii.), the baskets of figs (*Jer.* xxiv.), and Hosea's domestic grief (*Hosea* i.–iii.).

The classification of the book of *Job* among the parables of the Bible involves no assumption as to the historic reality—or otherwise—of the facts narrated. Whichever opinion be adopted the book remains a dramatized parable, with just enough of an epic element to serve as a kind of frame. The great problem of suffering innocence, treated reflectively in Psalm lxxiii., imaginatively in *Wisdom* v., is here treated dramatically with all the various elements of interest—character, action, background—which drama contributes. Here it will only be possible to point out how the book contains specimens of almost all the literary types which have been described above. There is first the epic element, which

The book of *Job.*

tells of Job as a man who as much excels his fellows in piety as he does in worldly prosperity. Upon this man there falls the hand of adversity, and almost at one blow he is bereft of family and goods and all that made life bright to him. Then, after a dirge in which he bemoans his lot and curses the day of his birth, his friends come to comfort him, and their advent inaugurates what may be entitled the philosophical element of the book. They come armed with the traditional theory that misfortune and suffering were always the punishment for sin—a theory which survived in the gospel age (*John* ix. 2)—and the keen, almost angry, discussion around this point forms the major part of the book. Epic and lyric elements in the book have already been noticed, and in this section there is lofty rhetoric as well as philosophy. Then, when Elihu had stated with vehemence the same theory in a modified form, "the Lord answered Job out of the whirlwind." It is not the least remarkable feature of this remarkable book that the final pronouncement on the great central question at issue is so utterly out of harmony with traditional Jewish opinion: for it is Job, and not his friends, who is declared to have said the thing that

was right. Finally, in a short epic section, full
of the peace that follows upon conflict, the narrative of the first two chapters is taken up ;
the prosperity of Job returns, his '' latter
end '' is blessed ''more than his beginning,''
until at last he dies, ''being old and full of
days.''

HISTORY—$\begin{Bmatrix} a \\ b \end{Bmatrix}$ Historical framework, running throughout the Bible.
Epic incidents ; sometimes single, sometimes in Cycles centering in an individual.

(c) Constitutional and Ecclesiastical History, containing the body of law which was to govern the nation's life, and also such narratives as bear upon the organization of the nation. This includes the greater part of the books of Exodus, Leviticus, Numbers, 1 and 2 Chronicles, Ezra, Nehemiah, and, in a slightly different sense, the four Gospels and the Acts.

(d) Rhetorical History. Panegyric on Famous Men (Ecclesiasticus xliv.–l. 24.).

LYRIC POETRY—(a) Elegies. Lament of David over Saul and Jonathan (2 Samuel i. 19–27); Song of the Exiles (Psalm cxxxvii.). Acrostic Elegies : Lamentations of Jeremiah.

(b) Hymns of Worship—(i.) General thanksgiving. Psalms cxlv.–cl., ciii., civ.
(ii.) Specific thanksgivings. Psalms cvii., cxviii.
(iii.) Private meditations. Psalms xiii., xiv., li., cxix.; the last being acrostic in the original.

(c) Special Odes—(i.) Military : Song of Deborah (Judges v.); of Miriam and Moses (Exodus xv.); of David (2 Samuel xxii.).
(ii.) Ceremonial : Of the bringing of the Ark to Jerusalem (Psalms xxiv., xxx., lxviii., cxxxii.).
(iii.) Private thanksgivings : Song of Hannah (1 Samuel ii. 1–10); of Habakkuk (Habakkuk iii.); of Mary, Zacharias, and Simeon (Luke i. and ii.).

(d) Dramatic Lyrics—Psalm cxxxix.
(e) Historical Odes—Psalms lxxviii., cv., cvi.; Deuteronomy xxxii.

TABLE OF LITERARY FORMS—*Continued.*

PHILOSOPHY—(*a*) { *f* } Prophetic Odes—Genesis xxvii.; Deuteronomy xxxiii.
{ *g* } Idyl—Song of Solomon.

The Proverb—sometimes taking the form of a riddle. Too numerous to call for references.

(*b*) Proverb-Simile—like the above but instituting a comparison.
(*c*) Proverb-Cluster—A group not organically combined but bearing on the same topic. Proverbs xxvi. 3-12.

(*d*) Essay—Systematic treatment of a topic. More common in Ecclesiasticus than in Proverbs. On Respect of Persons (James ii. 1-13); on Speech (iii. 1-12); on Times and Seasons (Ecclesiastes iii.-iv. 8).

(*e*) Monologue—The Cry of Wisdom (Proverbs i. 20-33; viii. 4-36).

PROPHECY—(*a*) Prophetic Address—The orations of Moses in Deuteronomy. The examples from the books of the prophets are too numerous to call for any reference.

(*b*) Prophecies of Doom or the Converse (Jeremiah xlvi.-li.; Isaiah xiii.-xxvii.).
(*c*) Image Prophecy (see below).
(*d*) Prophetic Rhapsody—partaking of the nature of History, Rhetoric, and Lyric Poetry (book of Joel).

PARABLE—(*a*) The Ordinary Parable—usually from nature. Parable of the Trees (Judges ix.); of the Ewe-lamb (2 Samuel xii.); of the Vineyard (Isaiah v.); also the parables of Jesus.

(*b*) Image Prophecy—(1) Dreams and Visions. Dream of Pharaoh (Genesis xli.); of Nebuchadnezzar (Daniel ii.-iv.); of Peter {Acts x.}.
(2) Emblem Prophecy. Emblem of the Girdle {Jeremiah xiii.}; the Basket of Figs (Jeremiah xxiv.).

(*c*) The Book of Job—a Dramatic Parable, contained in an epic frame, and comprising specimens of lyric, philosophic, rhetorical, and parabolic literature.

QUESTIONS.

1 What are the three stages in the history which makes the "framework" of Biblical literature?

2 What are the five main literary types recognizable in the books of Scripture? Show how the book of *Job* contains literature of more than one type.

3 What is meant by the word "epic"? Give an example of an Epic incident, and an Epic Cycle.

4 How do you explain the fact that certain parts of the Bible can be called either Constitutional or Ecclesiastical History? Do the Gospels come under this head?

5 Show the distinction between English and Biblical verse. Illustrate by quotations.

6 Give an example of each of the six kinds of lyrics in the Bible.

7 What is the leading interest in Psalm cxviii. as a piece of literature?

8 Show any special literary feature in Psalm cvii.

9 Why is Psalm cxxxix. called "dramatic"?

10 How does "Wisdom literature" differ from prophecy?

11 Give an example of a "Proverb-cluster" and an "Essay," and show what is the main difference between these two literary types.

47

12 What is the chief difference between *Ecclesiastes* and previous books of wisdom ?

13 Compare accounts of the Plagues of Egypt as given in *Exodus* and in *Wisdom.*

14 Explain the meaning of the word "prophecy."

15 Give the substance of the Oration of Moses in *Deuteronomy* xxviii.

16 Show the general drift of the book of *Joel.*

17 Give examples of parables in the Old Testament.

18 Give an example of a parabolic vision in the New Testament.

19 Explain and illustrate what is meant by "Emblem Prophecy."

20 Show that more than one view of the mystery of affliction falling upon the righteous is contained in the book of *Job.*

www.ingramcontent.com/pod-product-compliance
Lightning Source LLC
Chambersburg PA
CBHW031817090426
42739CB00008B/1306